Marriage Customs

Anita Compton

Thomson Learning

New York

Comparing Religions

Birth Customs
Death Customs
Food and Fasting
Initiation Customs
Marriage Customs
Pilgrimages and Journeys

About this book

This book looks at marriage customs in different religious traditions around the world. It describes different ceremonies and the significance of promises made and contracts signed by the couple getting married. The book shows that many rituals and symbols connected with marriage have their roots in basic principles about family life. Looking at various wedding celebrations can lead to an understanding of these fundamental beliefs.

First published in the
United States in 1993 by
Thomson Learning
115 Fifth Avenue
New York, NY 10003

First published in 1992 by
Wayland (Publishers) Ltd.

Cataloging-in-Publication Data applied for

ISBN: 1-56847-033-9

Printed in Italy

Contents

Words that appear in **bold** in the text are
explained in the glossary on page 30.

Introduction

A custom is something that people do at special times and on special occasions in a family, a religion, a country, or a society. Customs mark events to remember. This book will explore certain marriage customs. Some will be ordinary, but others

Below Couples who do not have arranged marriages go out together for some time to get to know each other before they get married.

Above A wedding is an occasion for families to come together. This Sikh couple are surrounded by members of their families, who join in the celebrations of their wedding day.

will be **sacred**, which means they carry religious messages.

Some customs are linked to new beginnings. Marriage is a new beginning for two people and is celebrated at a **ceremony** called a wedding. At a wedding, various customs show that the bride and groom are making an agreement to care for each other. They agree to share the ups and downs of life together. Certain words are said, and promises are made. Rings may be exchanged, scarves may be used to join the couple, hands may be held, or agreements may be signed as part of the ceremony. For people who have a religious ceremony, these customs are made sacred because they believe that their god is present to bless the marriage.

Choosing and finding a partner

The custom of choosing a person to marry varies from culture to culture. Customs are the ideas and ways of doing things in different societies. A society is made up of many people and groups.

In some groups, parents help their children find suitable partners. Lots of questions are asked, and when the right person is found the marriage is arranged. It is usual for Hindus, Muslims, and Sikhs to have arranged marriages.

Some people try to find a partner with the help of a computer service. This help is organized by special firms called dating services. They try to match women and men who are looking for someone to marry. In other groups, it is common for people to find their own partners by

Below Guests at a wedding procession in Sumatra are loaded with gifts that they will give to the bride and groom.

Tabira, a Muslim girl, describes a *mehndi* ceremony she went to: "A few days before the man and lady are married, there is a *mehndi* party. Everyone comes to the bride's house and the bride's hands and feet are painted with *mehndi* powder. Here the groom is being fed with sweets by the bride's family."

meeting people themselves. In whatever way people choose a partner, once they agree to get married, they are making the important decision to spend their lives with another person.

The wedding ceremony is a time of change. Two people give up being single and change over to become married. This means that there is a change of **status**. A women becomes a wife, and a man becomes a husband. Many women change their surnames and take on the last names of their husbands.

Inviting guests

Family and friends are usually invited to a wedding by the parents of the bride. A wedding is a special and happy occasion, and guests enjoy taking part in the celebrations. They are **witnesses** at the wedding service and often join in the wedding party afterward.

The wedding ceremony is very personal for the couple. It marks the beginning of their life together. But it is also a public event, because a lot of people see that the bride and groom are leaving their families to start a new life together.

In most religious traditions, marriage customs are organized around four important aspects. When you read about the customs in this book, you will find out which of these aspects they fit.

1. **Ritual** aspects. Rituals are actions that people perform as part of a ceremony. These rituals often carry a religious meaning. Some marriage rituals are performed by the couple, some by the guests, and some by the religious leader taking part in the ceremony. Christians have priests and ministers, Jews have a rabbi, Hindus have a priest, and Muslims have an imam. Sikhs are married in front of a special book called the Guru Granth Sahib.

2. **Symbolic** aspects. A symbol can be an action or a thing that has a special meaning. There are many symbolic marriage customs that have to do with the clothes worn, the foods eaten, and the objects (such as rings) that are used in the wedding ceremony. Symbols often hold religious meanings.

3. **Social** aspects. These are customs that have to do with the husband and wife living together. Social customs are different from group to group. They depend on the background, culture, and country that people come from.

4. **Legal** aspects. These are customs to do with the marriage contract and the promises made. A couple must have a marriage license to be married. Some couples will have a civil ceremony in City Hall. Others will have a religious ceremony. In some religious ceremonies, the couple sign a special book.

Above In England, signing the register at a Registry Office wedding makes the marriage legal.

Words and deeds

In religious ceremonies, some of the customs are rituals that are performed by the bride and groom and the leader taking part in the wedding service.

Promises, promises

A promise may be easy or hard to keep. Promises made at weddings are supposed to be kept for life.

At many weddings, you will hear couples making promises. Sometimes these promises are said out loud, sometimes the couple will sign a document, and sometimes both. The promises are important, so they are said or signed in the presence of the wedding guests. This shows that the couple intend to keep their promises so that

Right At this mixed Buddhist-Hindu wedding, the couple will vow to care for and be faithful to each other.

their marriage can work well. Some religious people believe that the promises are made in the presence of God. Although God is invisible, people believe that God is still aware of the marriage and knows the promises made by the two people.

Marriage as a sacrament

"Two into one doesn't go" is a principle in math. But Christians turn this idea upside down! In marriage, it is believed that two people become one in a special way. They are joined together in the sight of God.

Above This Asian Muslim bride is reading her wedding contract. She will tell the witnesses three times that she agrees to the wedding.

Right The Roman Catholic priest is giving wine to the bride during the wedding ceremony. She and her husband drink from the same cup. This shows that they will share their life, both the joys and the sad times.

Below After the rings have been blessed by the priest, the bride and groom exchange them. Here the groom is placing the ring on the third finger of the bride's left hand.

The bride and groom make **vows** that join them together for life. It is also believed that God joins the couple together through the priest. The marriage is more than a human agreement. Because they make the promises through the priest and before God, the promises are special and holy. The couple have another partner to give them strength in their marriage. This is God. Roman Catholics and Greek Orthodox Christians regard marriage as a **sacrament.**

Marriage vows
In many Christian weddings, the bride and groom promise to love each other "for better or worse, for richer or poorer, in sickness and in health" until they are parted by death. They each say these

11

words in front of the priest and loudly enough for the wedding guests to hear.

The bride and groom make their marriage vows when they give each other a ring. Each says:

"I give you this ring as a sign of our marriage
With my body I honor you
All that I am I give to you
All that I have I share with you
Within the love of God."

While it is usual for women to wear wedding rings and to change their last names, this has not always been the custom for men. Some people say that the custom of the bride's father "giving away" his daughter is unfair because it treats men and women very differently. In the past, this custom showed that women were the property of men. Most women today do not think so! Many modern brides do not follow the custom of being given away by their fathers, and they keep their own last names.

Promises in a Hindu marriage are made before God, who is believed to be present in the form of a special fire. The wedding ceremony is led by a priest, or brahmin. The couple make their vows in the form of a custom called *Satapadi*, which means Seven Steps. These are taken as they walk around the sacred fire pot four times. These steps help the bride and groom to see that in their

Below A Hindu bride and groom stand in front of the sacred fire before they take the Seven Steps.

12

Above A Hindu bride places a garland of flowers over her husband's head. This custom shows that the couple will honor and respect each other.

marriage they will walk together and carry out seven duties. After the seventh step, the bride and groom place their right hands on the their partner's heart. They do no sign anything. They believe their signatures are written by their feet and with invisible ink on their hearts. The bride and groom agree that they will:

1. earn a living to provide food;

2. work for power and strength so that they can stay healthy and be strong for each other;

3. care for the **welfare** of each other so that their marriage can grow and prosper;

4. be concerned about each other's happiness and pleasure;

5. hope for children, whom they will love and care for;

6. behave toward each other in an adaptable way and show that they can adjust to the other person, the place, and the time;

7. work for close union and friendship so that they can live together as good friends.

By taking these steps, they are making their vows.

At a Jewish wedding, the groom says these words to the bride as he puts a ring on her finger:

*"By this you are **consecrated** to me according to the law of Moses and Israel."*

The bride does not have to give or say anything to the groom. Accepting the ring is her way of showing that she agrees to marry him.

The meaning and duties of marriage

A Sikh wedding can be led by any Sikh woman or man who is well thought of in the community. This is usually a person with strong religious faith and knowledge. The ceremony is called *Anand Karaj*, which means "ceremony of bliss," and takes place in front of the Sikh holy book, the Guru Granth Sahib. This shows that the couple are seeking the help, grace, and blessing of God in their marriage. In a short talk, the leader

Sujata, a Hindu girl, describes her sister's wedding:
"The bride and groom both wore garlands made from flowers, and the bride had some beautiful jewelry. She wore special bracelets that our uncle gave her as a good luck present.
A bride can wear nine, eighteen, or thirty-six bracelets. My sister wore eighteen."

explains the sacred meaning of marriage. Two hearts should become one, joined by the light of Sikh teachings in the Guru Granth Sahib.

Duties of husbands and wives are brought to the couple's attention. They are asked to be faithful and loyal to each other, to celebrate each other's joys, and to be kind to one another in sorrow or pain. They are also asked to be kind, loving, and respectful to their relatives. The couple show that they agree to the marriage when they bow before the Guru Granth Sahib.

Four marriage hymns called *Lavan* are read. Between each hymn, musicians play while the bride and groom walk clockwise around the Guru Granth Sahib. This shows that they accept each other and the duties of marriage. Sometimes, the wedding guests throw bright flowers and petals at the couple

Right At a Sikh wedding, the couple are seated in front of the Guru Granth Sahib, the Sikh holy book.

Left Joined together by a pink scarf, this Sikh bride and groom are walking clockwise around the Guru Granth Sahib to make their wedding vows.

as they walk around the Guru Granth Sahib for the fourth and last time.

Buddhists have a ceremony that is not considered sacred. However, the groom and bride do make promises. They promise to be considerate to each other and to love, respect, and be faithful to one another. The man promises to provide gifts and presents to please his wife. The woman promises to be **hospitable** to her husband's family and friends. At the blessing of a Buddhist marriage by monks, the families promise to keep the five precepts, or laws. These precepts teach people that the way to happiness is to live a good life by not killing, stealing, lying, or drinking alcohol. Men and women also promise to be faithful to each other.

Buddhist monks and nuns live a life dedicated to the teachings of the Buddha and do not marry. Marriage is for **lay**

Above Buddhist monks do not marry. They live together in a community known as the *sangha*.

people; it is a social and not a religious occasion. Wedding customs vary according to the local community or culture.

Marriage contracts

At some weddings, agreements are made that help husbands and wives to be responsible to each other. These set out the needs and conditions that will create happiness for the couple.

The customs at Jewish wedding ceremonies depend on which branch of Judaism the bride and groom come from. Some will be **Orthodox** and some will be **Progressive** Jews.

Orthodox and some Progressive Jewish brides receive a *ketubah*, which is a marriage contract. It is a piece of paper like a certificate that is often beautifully decorated. The groom gives this to his

Right A Jewish groom is signing the marriage contract called the *ketubah*. It contains the duties and rules of care and "loving kindness" that he agrees to give his wife in their marriage.

bride before the marriage ceremony.

Traditionally, the *ketubah* contains the duties and care that the husband agrees to give his wife. The husband is obliged to provide food, clothes, and a home for his wife and children. The contract also contains rules that protect the wife and children in the event of death or divorce. A common practice today is for wives and husbands to set out the terms of the agreement together. Once signed, the contract binds the couple together.

The Koran, the Muslim holy book, gives guidance on family life. It requires that a contract be made between the two people who are marrying. The contract is thought of as a human, not a sacred, agreement. However, Muslims agree to live according to the teachings of Islam found in the Koran. The time when the contract is signed is called *Nikka*.

Muslims who come from Asia usually sign the marriage contract separately. The contract is taken by the imam to the groom, who signs it in the presence of four witnesses. Two witnesses must come from his family and two from the bride's family. Once the groom has signed, the contract is taken to the bride to sign. She says three times in front of the witnesses that she agrees to the marriage. The contract can be signed some time before the wedding ceremony or on the same day.

Above The families of this Muslim couple have gone to a lot of trouble to make sure that they have chosen the right partners for their children. During the wedding ceremony, the bride and groom agree to live together according to the teachings of their holy book, the Koran.

Signs and symbols

Symbols are actions or objects that represent, or stand for, something else. They often have a deep underlying meaning. For example, the sacred fire at a Hindu wedding is a symbol of the presence of the Radiant One. Fire and light are symbols of God's wisdom, truth, and justice. The fire at a Hindu wedding ceremony is the witness.

Right Four friends are holding a cloth on four poles over the Jewish bride and groom to make a chupah, a canopy they stand under when they make their promises to each other.

Many marriage customs include the use of signs and symbols. Jewish weddings take place under a canopy called a chupah. This sometimes looks like the roof of a tent on four poles. It is a symbol of the new home the bride and groom will make. The chupah poles are often decorated with flowers and ribbons.

Cups or glasses

While a Jewish bride and groom stand under the chupah, they drink from the same cup or glass of wine that has

Left The glass from which the bride and groom drink is stamped on and broken by the groom. Breaking and stamping on the glass is a sign that the wedding ceremony is completed. It reminds everyone present that love is fragile, and that there will be happy and sad times.

Ezra, a page boy at his teacher Miss Brown's wedding, says:
"In the synagogue, I remember the rabbi blessed the wine. Eden drank it first, and then Miss Brown took some and Eden stamped on the glass. I shouted *Mazel Tov*, which means good luck and be happy, as loud as I could. I had to wear nice clothes and all the grown-ups made a fuss over me."

been blessed. The ceremony ends with the breaking of the glass, which the groom stamps on. The broken glass is an important symbol. It suggests that love, like glass, is fragile and needs to be taken care of. It also reminds Jewish people of the time in history when their temple in Jerusalem was destroyed.

Throwing food

Barley or grains are a symbol of the harvest and fruitfulness. At some Orthodox Jewish weddings, grains are thrown at the bride, and a prayer is said that asks God to bless her and make her the mother of thousands. Rice is thrown at Hindu brides in hope that they will have many children.

Wearing veils

Many Jewish and Christian brides get married in veils that cover their faces. It is a custom for some Orthodox Jewish brides to have a special ceremony just as they enter the synagogue. The groom lifts up the bride's veil to make sure that he is marrying the right woman.

This custom is practiced because of a story in the book of Genesis about Jacob and Rachel. Jacob worked. for a man called Laban, because he was in love with his daughter Rachel. He asked Laban if he could marry Rachel, but Laban tricked Jacob by giving him a veiled bride. She turned out to be Rachel's older sister Leah.

Wedding clothes

It is a custom for Jewish and Christian brides to wear a white or cream wedding dress. White is a symbol of purity. Jewish men wear a skull cap called a yarmulke and a white **tallith**, or prayer shawl, at their wedding. It is a custom for men to be buried in a tallith, so this is both a symbol of joy and of mourning.

Below The groom is lifting the veil to make sure he has the right bride. He does not want to end up like Jacob and marry the wrong woman!

Right This Hindu bride from Nepal is wearing the traditional red sari embroidered with gold threads and beautiful gold jewelry.

Asian brides, whether Hindu, Muslim, or Sikh, usually get married in a red or deep pink-colored silk, embroidered with gold threads. Red is considered to be a happy, bright color that is appropriate for a wedding, an occasion of excitement and joy. Hindu brides wear a sari and a long scarf called a *chunni* to cover the head. It is usual for Muslim and Sikh brides to wear special clothes called *shalwar* and *kameeze*, with a long scarf called a *dupatta*. A *kameeze* is a long, elegant, and beautifully embroidered tunic worn over loose or baggy trousers called *shalwar*.

Asian men get married in their own traditional dress, either an Indian suit or a western suit. A long white jacket with a stand-up collar is often worn over white trousers. Sikhs wear **turbans** that are often a deep red color, while Hindu men sometimes wear a special hat called a *tupi*, a turban decorated with a feather, sequins, or jewels to look like a crown.

Left Behind his *kalgri*, or face mask, the Sikh bridegroom wears a dark red turban.
He is also wearing a pink scarf that will be used as a symbol to join him with the bride.

Above Bridesmaids and page boys dress up to follow the bride on her wedding day.

Right Wedding rings are worn by the bride and groom to show they they will give their love to each other forever. The Christian custom of placing
wedding rings on the third finger of the left hand grew from
the belief that the third
finger contains a vein that goes directly to the heart.

Bridesmaids and page boys

Although you will see bridesmaids and page boys who attend the bride at many weddings, this custom is not a religious one. But it shows that the bride is special on her wedding day.

Rings

Wedding rings are often plain. Usually they are smooth gold bands that have no beginning and no end. Rings are like circles of love that have no beginning and no end, so they are thought of as symbols of **eternity**. They show that the couple belong together and hope to stay together for life.

After the blessing at a Jewish wedding, the groom places a plain wedding ring on the index finger of the bride's right hand. The custom requires that

something valuable should be given to the bride. It is not necessary to give a ring, but it is the usual custom. Whatever is given is placed on the bride's right hand. Two witnesses must be present, and placing the ring on the right index finger makes it easier for the witnesses to see.

Painting patterns on hands and feet

At many Asian weddings, whether Hindu, Muslim, or Sikh, the bride will have beautiful patterns painted on her hands and the soles of her feet. This is a social and not a religious custom. The patterns are painted with a powder made from the crushed leaves of the *mehndi* tree. This powder turns the skin a warm red color.

Left This Muslim bride's hands are decorated with *mehndi* patterns for her wedding day.

At Hindu weddings, after the couple have taken the Seven Steps, it is the custom for the groom to paint the bride's hairline or part red. This is a sign that the woman is now married and that she belongs to her husband and his family.

Above Having a special meal after the ceremony is a traditional marriage custom. Food is being served to the wedding guests at this reception in Pakistan.

Special food

At most wedding parties there is special food. For Christians it is a custom to have a wedding cake. The cake is usually covered with white icing, and sometimes it has three tiers, or levels. Traditionally, the couple are expected to save one level of their wedding cake to celebrate their first anniversary.

After the ceremony

After some Hindu wedding ceremonies, there is a custom that the bride and groom go home, eat, and play what is called "the ring game." The priest puts a ring in a tank of red-colored water with rice and stones in it. The bride and groom have to find the ring three or more times. The person who finds it more times is said to be the ruler of the house.

There is also the custom that the bride is **ransomed** by her sisters. Because of this, the bridegroom has to give rings or presents to the sisters of the bride before he can take her to his family.

At a **Greek Orthodox** wedding party there is music, and the bride and groom often dance with a white scarf between them.

When a couple finally leaves after all the wedding celebrations, they begin their new life together. Brides in all traditions leave in new clothes. Sometimes the bride's parents buy these for her. A Hindu bride leaves the wedding in special clothes bought for her by her husband's family.

Sikh weddings often end with a farewell ceremony called *Doli*. The mother and sisters of the bride dress her in new clothes and jewelry and say

Alexis went to a Greek Orthodox wedding:
"At the very end they pin a lot of money onto the couple's clothes for their honeymoon – it's got to be a ten-dollar bill or over. People give what they can, but often fifty- and hundred-dollar bills are pinned on the bride's dress. Anyway, they get a lot of money."

goodbye. The bridegroom then takes her away to his family home in a brightly decorated car.

One custom that sometimes takes place after a Christian wedding is "crossing the threshold." The man carries his bride over the threshold, or doorway, of their new home. Doors are important symbols. When a couple "cross the threshold" they are entering their new life together.

Married life often begins with a vacation or a honeymoon. This is a time when the newlyweds get to know each other better and make plans for their future together.

Below Together and alone at last! Newlyweds leave on a ship to begin their journey to their secret honeymoon place.

Glossary

Ceremony A formal act often carried out as part of a custom.

Consecrated Dedicated to something or someone in particular.

Eternity Endless time.

Hospitable Welcoming to visitors.

Lay people People who are not religious leaders.

Legal To do with the law.

Greek Orthodox Members of the division of the Christian church mainly based in eastern Europe.

Orthodox Jews Jews who strictly follow the teachings God revealed to the prophet, Moses.

Progressive Jews Jews who believe that the teachings of Moses can be adapted to the modern world.

Ransomed Held as a prisoner until money is paid for a person's release.

Ritual To do with carrying out religious services in a set way.

Sacrament Something that is believed to have a special religious significance.

Sacred Holy or relating to God.

Sari Traditional dress of women in India, Pakistan, and surrounding countries. It is a long, narrow piece of cloth wrapped around the body.

Social To do with people and society.

Status A person's position in society.

Symbolic Standing for something else.

Tallith A white prayer shawl worn by Jewish men.

Turban A man's headdress, which is a long length of cloth wrapped around the head.

Vows Solemn promises.

Welfare Well-being.

Witnesses People who see an event happen.

Books to read

Barbarians, Christians, and Muslims (Minneapolis: Lerner Publications, 1975)

Buddhist Festivals (Vero Beach, Fl.: Rourke Corp., 1987)

Christian Celebrations for Autumn & Winter (Carthage, Ill.: Good Apple, 1990)

Jewish Days and Holidays (Bellmore, N.Y.: Adama Publications, 1986)

Many Children: Religions Around the World (Reston, Va.: M.A. Thomas, 1987)

Religion and Society (Milwaukee: Gareth Stevens Inc., 1991)

Sikh Festivals (Vero Beach, Fl.: Rourke Corp., 1993)

Picture Acknowledgments

The publishers wish to thank the following for supplying the photographs in this book:
Cephas Picture Library 11 (top, Frank B. Higham, bottom, Mick Rock), 28 (Helen Stylianou); Chapel Studios 5 (Zul Mukhida); Eye Ubiquitous 6 (left, P.M. Feild), 8, 12 (Helene Rogers), 13 (Helen Rogers); Hutchison Library cover, 10 (Christine Pemberton), 20 (Liba Taylor), 22 (Liba Taylor), 24, 29 (Robert Francis); Ann & Bury Peerless 15, 16 (top); Tony Stone Worldwide 16 (Hilarie Kavanagh), 23 (David Hanson); Wayland Picture Library 4, 18, 26, 27; ZEFA 14, 17, 19, 25 (both).

Index

Numbers in **bold** indicate photographs.